PIGS!

A MY INCREDIBLE WORLD PICTURE BOOK

MY INCREDIBLE WORLD

Copyright © 2018, My Incredible World

All rights reserved. This book or any portion thereof may not be reproduced or used in any manner whatsoever without the express written permission of the copyright holder.

www.myincredibleworld.com

Photos Licensed Under CC BY 2.0. Full terms at https://creativecommons.org/licenses/by/2.0:
Page 2. "こぶた" by kagawa_ymg, available at https://www.flickr.com/photos/7284762@N07/2953005313
Page 3. "Pig" by Sam Howzit, available at https://www.flickr.com/photos/aloha75/14853079844
Page 4. "the wise eyes of a pig" by Ryan, available at https://www.flickr.com/photos/ryanready/4673886670
Page 8. "Different Pigs" by Arran Moffat, available at https://www.flickr.com/photos/arran_moffat/9397640906
Page 11. "Different Pigs" by Arran Moffat, available at https://www.flickr.com/photos/arran_moffat/9394868309
Page 12. "Pig at Ardenwood" by Amit Patel, available at https://www.flickr.com/photos/amitp/7650447292
Page 13. "A Pig, Snuffling" by Alistair Young, available at https://www.flickr.com/photos/ajy/15676615032

Photos Licensed Under CC BY-SA 2.0. Full terms at https://creativecommons.org/licenses/by-sa/2.0:
Page 5. "DSC01806" by Meg Stewart, available at https://www.flickr.com/photos/megstewart/5607864929
Page 9. "Greenfield Village 2015" by F. D. Richards, available at https://www.flickr.com/photos/50697352@N00/18388584528
Page 10. "20160804-P8040012" by Martin Robson, available at https://www.flickr.com/photos/martinrobson/29057388666

Photos Licensed Under CC0 1.0. Full terms at https://creativecommons.org/publicdomain/zero/1.0/deed.en:
Page 1. Untitled by Alexas_Fotos, available at https://pixabay.com/en/piglet-small-pigs-mini-cute-sweet-3279496
Page 6. Untitled by Snap_it, available at https://pixabay.com/en/pot-bellied-pig-pig-fat-tired-2413454
Page 7. "Kunekune Cuteness" by Paul Rowe, available at https://www.flickr.com/photos/armchaircaver/4468567199
Page 17. Untitled by filinecek, available at https://pixabay.com/en/pig-piggy-bank-wild-boar-animal-3033965
Page 18. Untitled by Gellinger, available at https://pixabay.com/en/animal-pig-piglet-pink-curly-tail-2530930
Page 19. Untitled by minka2507, available at https://pixabay.com/en/miniature-pig-animal-farm-3097255
Page 20. Untitled by Alexas_Fotos, available at https://pixabay.com/en/piglet-young-animals-pig-small-2782611
Page 21. Untitled by Alexas_Fotos, available at https://pixabay.com/en/pig-lying-sun-farm-animal-cozy-2189566
Page 22. Untitled by bjtiller0, available at https://pixabay.com/en/nature-animal-mammal-wildlife-wild-3258810

Other Photos Credits:
Page 14. Untitled by Jakob Owens, available at https://unsplash.com/photos/bEwKUiMvsLM
Page 15. Untitled by Christopher Carson, available at https://unsplash.com/photos/i4XLJmlYit4
Page 16. Untitled by Annie Spratt, available at https://unsplash.com/photos/E97AP-KmemE

Pigs live all over the world except in Antarctica.

Pigs have an extraordinary sense of smell!

There are hundreds of different breeds of pigs!

Pigs have poor eyesight, but they see in color, like us.

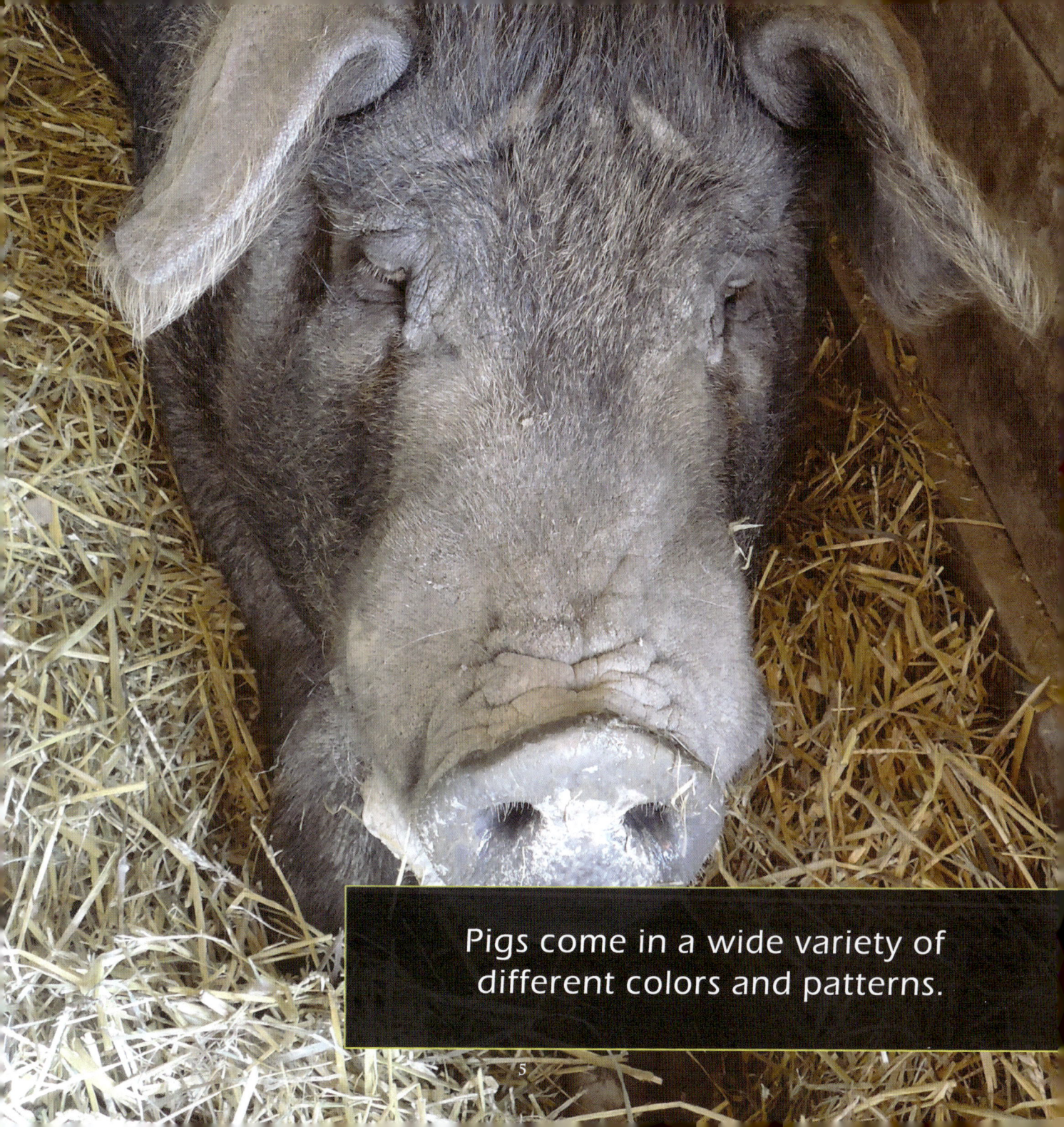

Pigs come in a wide variety of different colors and patterns.

Pigs can weigh up to 770 pounds (350 kg)!

Baby pigs are called **piglets**.

Pigs are very curious and may be as smart as a 3-year-old human!

Pigs are **omnivorous**, meaning they eat both plants and meat.

Pigs sleep about 9 to 11 hours per day!

Pigs are some of the cleanest animals around!

Pigs roll around in mud to keep cool!

Pigs have better hearing than humans!

There are pigs in the Bahamas that are famous for swimming in the ocean!

Mother pigs usually have litters of 8 to 12 piglets.

Wild pigs live mainly in forests.

Pigs talk to each other using grunts, oinks, snarls, snorts, and squeaks!

Piglets can respond to their own names by around 20 days old!

Pigs have about 15,000 tastebuds! Humans only have around 10,000.

Some pigs have curly tails and others have straight ones!

Pigs can drink up to 14 gallons (53 L) of water every day!

Pigs are incredible!

Printed in Great Britain
by Amazon